A KANGAROO JOEY GROWS UP

by Joan Hewett

photographs by Richard Hewett

LERNER PUBLICATIONS COMPANY/MINNEAPOLIS

In His Mother's Pouch

Lick, lick.

A kangaroo cleans her pouch.

Soon her baby will be born.

The kangaroo lives in a nature preserve.
Hunting is not allowed here.
Life is peaceful.

A baby kangaroo is called a joey.

This joey's name is Kipper.

Kipper is no bigger than a kidney bean.

He has no fur.

He does not look like a kangaroo.

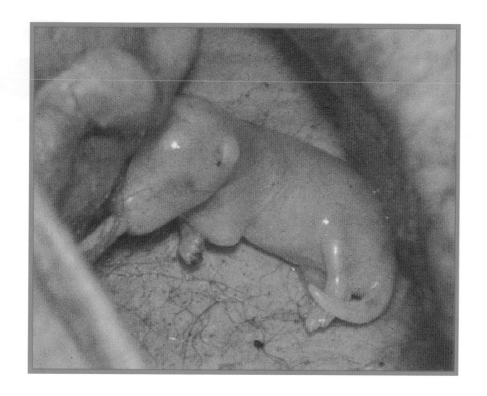

Kipper lives in his mother's pouch.

He drinks her milk.

He grows.

He begins to look like a kangaroo.

Kipper begins to move around.
When he is 6 months old, he peeks out.

Kipper hears a new noise.

He is afraid.

He hides his face in his mother's pouch.

Still, Kipper is curious.

He peeks out again.

Kipper sees other kangaroos!

LEARNING
TO HOP

Kipper is almost 8 months old.
He wants to stand on his own.

Slowly, the joey sets
his front legs down.
He climbs out
of the pouch.
He is on the ground.

Kipper has a long, heavy tail.
He has big back feet.
Kipper's tail and feet help him stand.
He looks around.

But Kipper's legs are not
strong enough to hop.
So he springs head-first
into his mother's pouch.

Then the joey somersaults.
And . . .

Lickety-split!

He is back in place.

Every day Kipper climbs out of the pouch.
Every day his legs get stronger.

Soon he can hop.

Hopping is hard work.
Kipper is tired.
He rests
in his mother's pouch.

From his front-row seat, Kipper sees his world.
His mother has strong legs.
She can hop all day without stopping.

KANGAROOS ABOUND

It is early in the morning.

Kangaroos are grazing.

Kipper is 10 months old.
He eats grass too.

Kipper stays close to his mother.
They move along slowly.

By noon, the air is hot.

Leafy trees provide shade.

Kipper licks his fur.

He feels cooler.

In the afternoon,
it is even hotter.
Kipper dives into
his mother's pouch.

His mother lies down.
They take a long nap.

ALMOST GROWN-UP

Kipper is 13 months old.
He hops easily.
But he cannot keep up
with his mother.

The big joey no longer fits
in his mother's pouch.
Still, he drinks her milk.
And wherever his mother goes,
Kipper tags along.

Kipper is 14 months old.
His back legs keep getting stronger.
Before long, he can hop as far
and as fast as his mother.

He can live on his own.

The kangaroo joey has grown up.

Birth	4 months old	6 months old
Kipper is the size of a pea. He lives in his mother's pouch. He drinks her milk.	Kipper begins to look like a kangaroo.	Kipper peel out of the po

More about Kangaroos

Kangaroos carry their babies in pouches. Animals that have pouches are called marsupials.

Kangaroos live in Australia. Australia is halfway around the world, south of the equator. Kipper is a gray kangaroo. Gray kangaroos live all over the continent of Australia.

When explorers from Europe first came to Australia, they were amazed. They had never seen large animals that hopped like grasshoppers. They had never seen animals that carried their young in pouches.

Later on, people from other countries settled in Australia. They cleared land to make way for sheep ranching. Good grazing land for sheep was also good grazing land for kangaroos. Kangaroos ate well on the ranches. The well-fed kangaroos had healthy babies. Soon there were more and more kangaroos.

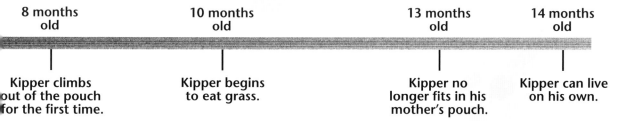

8 months old	10 months old	13 months old	14 months old
Kipper climbs out of the pouch for the first time.	Kipper begins to eat grass.	Kipper no longer fits in his mother's pouch.	Kipper can live on his own.

Thousands of kangaroos still roam wild in Australia. They hop across the desertlike outback. They leap over tall grass. They leap across roads. Signs tell drivers to watch out for kangaroos. Some Australians think there are too many kangaroos. Some hunters shoot the animals for sport.

Nature Preserves

Kipper and the other kangaroos in this book live at the Lone Pine Koala Sanctuary in Brisbane, Australia. It is a nature preserve. The animals that live there are protected from hunters. They have enough room to hop and leap. At Lone Pine, the kangaroos live a life that is similar to the life they would lead in the wild.

To Orson Ridgely Hewett, our first grandchild

Additional photos are reproduced by permission of: Zoological Society of San Diego, p. 5; © Jean-Paul Ferrero/Auscape, p. 6; © Inga Spence/Visuals Unlimited, p. 12.

This book is available in two editions:
Library binding by Lerner Publications Company,
  a division of Lerner Publishing Group, Inc.
Soft cover by First Avenue Editions,
  an imprint of Lerner Publishing Group, Inc.
241 First Avenue North
Minneapolis, MN 55401 U.S.A.

Website address: www.lernerbooks.com

Library of Congress Cataloging-in-Publication Data

Hewett, Joan.
  A kangaroo joey grows up / by Joan Hewett ; photographs by Richard Hewett.
     p.   cm.
    ISBN-13: 978–1–57505–165–9 (lib. bdg. : alk. paper)
    ISBN-10: 1–57505–165–6 (lib. bdg. : alk. paper)
    ISBN-13: 978–0–8225–0091–9 (pbk. : alk. paper)
    ISBN-10: 0–8225–0091–4 (pbk. : alk. paper)
    1. Kangaroos—Infancy—Juvenile literature. [1. Kangaroos. 2. Animals—Infancy.] I. Hewett, Richard, ill. II. Title.
    QL737.M35 H49   2002
    599.2'22—dc21   00-011448

Manufactured in the United States of America
8 9 10 11 12 13 – DP – 13 12 11 10 09 08

BABY ANIMALS

Kipper is a kangaroo joey. He is growing up in a nature preserve. Kipper lives in his mother's pouch. One day, he crawls out. It is time for Kipper to learn to hop. Find out about Kipper in *A Kangaroo Joey Grows Up.*

BABY ANIMALS BOOKS:

A FLAMINGO CHICK GROWS UP **A KOALA JOEY GROWS UP**

A HARBOR SEAL PUP GROWS UP **A TIGER CUB GROWS UP**

A KANGAROO JOEY GROWS UP

" . . . attractive and will enhance science collections."
—*School Library Journal*

"The short sentences, large print, and simple vocabulary are just right for new readers. Color photos on every page help draw children into the text."
—*Booklist*

ISBN 978-0-8225-0091-9

50695

9 780822 500919

FIRST AVENUE EDITIONS
AN IMPRINT OF LERNER PUBLISHING GROUP
www.lernerbooks.com